Allegedly
John Bourdeaux S.F.A. Cambs M.B.

Best wishes
John

Dedication

To Tean, Archie and Sophie whose love and humour makes life
a wonderful experience, indeed who knows,
one might continue the pottery tradition?

Allegedly

Printed & Published by:
The St Ives Printing & Publishing Company,
High Street, St Ives, Cornwall TR26 1RS, UK.

ISBN 978-0-948385-97-1

'Happiness is not in the mere
possession of money,
It lies in the joy of achievement,
In the thrill of creative effort.'

Allegedly
A Series of Innate Ramblings of a
Fairly Eccentric Island Potter

John Bourdeaux

Acknowledgements

A very sincere thanks to the many wonderful and diverse range of visitors who have supported the pottery since it's opening in May 1978.

It has been such a privilege to have met you all and, indeed, the friendships formed have been long lasting. This year we have had several delightful young people who are the fourth generation to grace our doors.

This book relates just a few of the stories that many of you may remember and, indeed, several new ones.

All of the stories without exception are based on fact, but I have taken the liberty of changing some names, to avoid embarrassment – or in this ridiculous modern age of political correctness – 'prosecution' hence the title *Allegedly*.

As always thanks to my wonderful wife and best friend of forty eight years, Margaret, a very very special person.

To Tean, Archie and Sophie whose love and humour makes life a wonderful experience, indeed who knows, one might continue the pottery tradition?

Additional Thanks ...

To survive forty years as a potter in the Isles of Scilly, has been a great experience.

I hope this small edition gives you some idea of the challenges and extreme humour that the various incidents described have provided. Each day is a new experience and one never knows what is likely to occur or, indeed, have no idea if any sales will be made. So sometimes one is dejected and at other times one is elated.

One constant: the great people who come to Scilly, new and old. The pottery welcomes you all.

Thanks for reading

John

Contents

The Author

IN APRIL 1978 John Bourdeaux decided to open his pottery in a very derelict barn at Old Town St Mary's.

With the help of a very helpful land steward for the Duchy of Cornwall a freehold purchase was made for this derelict shell of a building, planning permission eventually gained, the local boatmen, Mike Hicks, Mark Groves and Louis Hitchens helped to make the building fairly watertight. With the help of John Knott a government minister of the time, the south west electricity board reluctantly connected us.

The pottery opened with great apprehension on May 15th 1978.

Many challenges occurred ... but suffice it to say here we are in 2018 still really enjoying the fantastic way of life that the pottery has provided for Margaret and I and our two super boys Andrew and Ben.

I do hope you enjoy the short stories that follow in this book.

Golden Tern

Cold Feet, 2018

${\cal D}$enver

Misshapen Masterpieces & the Mighty Atom

WHILST ON MY SHORT sojourn at art college (eight weeks) I despaired at the lack of business understanding by the very talented students.

In 1962 I attended St Martins (now the central school of art) in London, however I studied at the business college situated at the time on the upper floors, but sharing many of the facilities with the art students, even in those days few of the very talented artists ever made any impact onto the vagaries of the art world. Many turning to primary and secondary teaching roles.

While at college, this time an art student myself, I decided to offer my business experience to my fellow students, primarily on how to obtain an exhibition, to show ones talents to a wider audience. They in turn helped me to master the art of the potter's wheel and simple glaze recipes, kiln firing etc. I had been accepted for a full years course at Bournemouth and Poole college of art. But due to family illness I only managed just short of one term. However, the lecturers were great, and the ceramic technician fantastic. Indeed it was with great sadness that I failed to complete the course. Returning home to Scilly, with the help of many local people we managed to get my very very derelict barn watertight and services installed. The family business was sold to an avaricious young islander and all the proceeds went to fund my parents' well earned retirement …

This accomplished, with a float of fifty pounds and six months rent loaned by my fantastic parents we set off to conquer the art world. Making a range of wheel thrown neo modernist sculptures all with intellectual sounding names and very different designs to the norm. Working on the principle that if it's different enough, one can like or dislike but not compare. However despite this self confessed genius I had yet to sell a pot and had the challenge to feed my wonderful young family, also excited by our vows of poverty and new challenges. Many locals despaired and those who weren't vocal at the incredibility of our actions, found it difficult to meet my eye in the local Co-Op.

This was about to radically change ... In early May 1978 before the studio had opened displaying all my misshapen masterpieces, I was struggling at the potter's wheel when Margaret entered looking rather anxious ... "I've just had a phone call from Penzance in Cornwall, an American gentleman from Denver Colorado, received your letter offering him to exhibit your works in Colorado and was so intrigued has flown over especially to see you and arrange the possibility of representing your world famous masterpieces".

Holy holy rhinoserae. How could this be ... the studio not yet opened, and I never yet having made a sale ... I now remembered teaching the students in Bournemouth on how to secure an exhibition, do not be self deprecating when offering your wares, be confident, success breeds success. Indeed I now faintly remember writing this fictitious spiel. Romanticising my non existent talents. How did this ever get to Colorado.

My delightful and lovely mother in law 'Violet', all four feet ten of her (known by the boys as the mighty atom) had inadvertently, trying as always to be extra helpful, addressed and posted the letter to the Banbury Fair gallery in Denver.

Hence the visit of two charming and discerning Americans, to our as yet unopened gallery.

The next day arrived ... Two immaculate Americans being met by Margaret and given an Island tour, then meeting me for lunch before the visit to the world famous studio. Probably the biggest challenge my salesmanship and personality had ever encountered. The strategy being, several large Bristol Cream sherries, followed by high quality wines, always a success in my past business lunches when working in Knightsbridge. Alas, would you believe it? They were very strict teetotallers, and indeed the demon drink was evil.

However, I had cleverly placed several pots into the new kiln and warmed them up ... allowing the gallery owners to open the kiln door and enjoy the delight of freshly fired pots. This made a great impression and never having encountered such a range of diverse misshapen masterpieces, soon realised that they were in the presence of pure genius !!!!! Once again luck on my side and indeed the strategy of making a very differing range of sculpture had paid off. A large order ensued, and for the next few months my wonderful customers enjoyed seeing all the packed tea chests off on their travels. So the newly initiated Island potter, now exhibiting in the States, and being interviewed on radio Denver.

I was finally given permission to have an open air exhibition in Tamarac Square in Denver, but declined ... always quit while you're ahead ... now forty years later I wonder where some of those masterpieces are, several hundred thousands of pots later.

All thanks to 'Violet', the mighty atom.

Africa, 2016

Brief Incidents

The Potters' Simple Lifestyle

THE FOLLOWING ARE A few brief happenings that are worthy of note in the potters' simple lifestyle in his studio at Old Town St Mary's, Isles of Scilly.

August 21st 1998

Today I was quietly making some pots on the wheel when rudely interrupted by a flushed overweight woman asking for the potter. She unfortunately had a piercing Home Counties accent which could well have lured many a ship to a watery grave. Sadly her appearance was that of a Patagonian goat herder (I have met a few in my travels, but none as bombastic as this individual) however telling her brood of four children, to be quite while she talked to the potter chappie.

Her opening salvo was that she had four weeks timeshare on Tresco and that all her intelligent children went to private schools who all had splendid ceramic departments. I soon found out the reason for this unwelcome disturbance of my peaceful existence.

She was going horse riding with the St Mary's Riding School and would be leaving the children with me for a couple of hours, a drink and a biscuit at eleven would suffice their needs and indeed they would help without pay. Flabbergasted and speechless I struggled to find an appropriate reply to this ghastly spectacle of womanhood.

How could I solve this dilemma … without giving offence?

I had recently seen a television programme of Jethro the Cornish comedian … attack being the best form of defence. Having not yet spoken, I foolishly went into my best peasant mode … inarticulate and a very broad Cornish accent … "Well Mrs, I be quite busy, but if you fancy a bit of friendly slap and tickle I be sure we can cum to sum other arrangement …

It worked … she never returned … heaven help those poor horses.

Rhinoceros

Resurrection

A Small Ceramic Puffin

TODAY ONCE AGAIN I regret the tendency I have to put people at their ease at all times. I've just had a long conversation with a really nice couple from Pinner in Middlesex, it is their first visit to the islands. We bring happy greetings from some very old mutual friends. They had promised that whatever happened they would visit the studio with a small gift for me.

To be honest I couldn't quite place the acquaintances that they were talking about, but rather than be rude I continued the conversation. I was sure that I soon would remember our friendship and their names. I have always prided myself on my excellent long-term memory, short term however not quite so good. However as the conversation progressed few clues came to give me an idea of who we were talking about, indeed little came forward to enlighten me of our past friendship. I was delighted to hear how well that their children had done in academia, indeed far surpassing their parents' expectations and aspirations, we discussed many other family members, their relationships, illnesses hardships and several other personal matters, unusually I still had no idea of who the mystery friends were so eventually and reluctantly I brought the extended conversation to an end, still in the dark as to who their friends were.

I reciprocated their generous gesture of the present to me, by sending back to Pinner, with the friends a small ceramic Puffin sculpture and an inscribe pottery pen as is the norm. So with firm handshakes and a big hug they departed, pausing at the door for final goodbye, saying, it was so nice to meet you, Humfrey.

As many of you know, my name is John, alas my dear friend Humfrey died several years ago!!! A clear case of mistaken identity, should I enlighten them, perhaps not, Humfrey was, for many years, a fantastic potter on the Garrison, St Mary's – a true gentleman and a great practical joker in his time, he would certainly have enjoyed this incident. Indeed he played many a joke on me, and would certainly have appreciated what had just occurred.

Once again he had got one up on me even from the grave.

Trio of Cormorants

Hairy Potter 4

Vows of Extreme Poverty

NO, I WAS NOT always a bearded scruffy artist, for many years before becoming a craftsman I suffered morning suits whilst working in Knightsbridge, collar and tie every day when running the family business in the Parade St Mary's, moonlighting as the local estate agent and running the Bristol and West building society on the island. Indeed a very, very, traditional and establishment type of person.

However I was informed by Alan Hicks, a Scillonian born and an old friend who was helping to get the pottery ready to open, that he and many other islanders were fairly apprehensive at my decision to take vows of extreme poverty and become a potter. Well John, if you have any hope of succeeding you have to alter this clean cut image you portray, why not start by growing a beard and wearing clothes that show your artistic roots, you may then have some chance of selling the odd (being the operative word) pot.

So thanks to Alan now forty years later I am still a scruffy git who has happily survived as a potter with a difference, with the help of a fantastic bunch of visitors and locals who have supported us (sincere thanks). To the cynics and doubters who still abound, really, really sorry to have disappointed you so far.

One short note to end on, after a few short months of making pots with a difference i.e. misshapen masterpieces (that now command a good price at auctions) I found that my new identity of the eccentric artist did have its drawbacks. One morning a forty year old holiday home owner came to the studio to buy a large number of pots, she informed me that her husband was having an affair and to punish him she was maxing out his credit card. I was obviously happy to oblige, such a purchase would see us through the next week. However my delight and appreciation was misinterpreted, invading my personal space she importunately suggested that a physical friendship would be welcomed and reciprocated.

Terrified and reverting to my former establishment self I had to reject this unwelcome advance without losing the sale, my dilemma was saved by my dear Margaret with the boys bringing me my morning coffee (in fact Valium would have been more appropriate). I sat thinking should I shave off the beard, definitely not Margaret advised as she found the whole episode extremely funny. The beard has stayed and no more incidents have occurred.

Abstracted Golden Pheasant, 2005

Faroe Islands

May 3rd 2007

TODAY WAS THE BANK Holiday weekend when the Islands host the World Gig Rowing Championships. Over one hundred crews come to the Islands from all over the world. To race for the most coveted trophy, in gig racing, a fine bunch of young people take over the Islands. Several thousand people crew and supporters enjoy the rowing, and indeed the local hostelries are full to overflowing until the early hours of the mornings.

Today is Monday and Gerry Twynham who owns the local bus called Katie has called into the pottery with thirty people on his Island tour. Four strapping youngsters, a picture of fitness dominate, in front of the counter, my gosh they are fit with rippling muscles and short cropped hair. Gerry explains that they come from the Faroe Islands, I start to make conversation with these rather humourless individuals. Spying one of my sculptures of an Icelandic bird on a shelf I ask. "Tell me, I gather you eat seabirds including the puffin"

A hush follows from the rest of the tour group, rapidly picking up on the conversation. "Yes we eat many of them, it is part of our culture" a hush falls on the tour group mainly comprising of National Trust and RSPB people over on a day trip from Cornwall. Continuing the conversation, "So what do they taste like" I ask tentatively. "Well they taste very much like the guillemots and razorbills" They reply in terse-broken English.

I desperately tried to keep the conversation going, mainly to interest the rest of the passengers. One last question and then perhaps they would move on and allow the rest to make some purchases, which I desperately needed. Inspired I ask "tell me, how did your ladies team do this year? I gather they are a really fit bunch".

A tense wait of several seconds, and then the largest and fittest replies "WE ARE THE LADIES TEAM"!!!!!

The coach driver crying with laughter at my embarrassment and indeed in true English fashion, the others smiling and pretending the conversation hadn't occurred. Sadly no purchases today, embarrassment all around.

Vase, 2004

Island Hotel

Neanderthal Hurrah Henry

WE WERE ALL SADDENED a few years ago at the closing of the Island hotel on the Island of Tresco on the Isles of Scilly. Amongst its guests was a vast range of superior families, very rich and indeed they portrayed a view of Britain that few of us knew existed. Usually rapid breeders with numerous ill mannered children, loud Oxbridge voices and the females of the species showing a great resemblance to emaciated turkeys.

However we all enjoyed lunching at this fabulous hotel not only because of the fabulous food and setting, but the bonus of people watching. To see the nouveau riche and the aristocracy behaving in bazaar and pretentious ways. The staff well accustomed to this objectionable behaviour have their own tales to tell of their subtle revenge.

A few years before the hotel finally closed I had a phone call from the manager whom I knew well, and considered a friend. "I have a family of extremely well heeled guests who are desperate to visit your studio". Alas this was on a Saturday and we have always closed on weekend afternoons for well earned family time, why live in this paradise and not enjoy it? – so Saturdays are sacrosanct.

The weather was slightly inclement so after a begging plea to help him out, and to heighten his chances of a good tip, I reluctantly agreed to open the studio especially at 2pm that afternoon. He would arrange a taxi to coincide with the hotel boat, to arrive at the studio at the allotted time. I waited with anticipation, looking forward to a good sale that would make up for the inconvenience of a special opening, indeed as the weather was fairly dismal perhaps this was not so much of an imposition.

2 pm arrived ... The taxi pulled up, and a six foot three Neanderthal hurrah Henry hammered on the door, in booming voice he shouts "Are you there Potter?" The door not being locked or even fully closed seemed to escape his Eton intelligence (or lack of it). However with the correct amount of subservience essential in these situations, I opened the door with a welcoming smile.

"Before we start I need to make something clear" he pronounces. "What now I think, usually the form is, do the peasants take credit cards. Indeed I think to myself, no problem, even Amex is taken here ... However what happens next was not quite as expected ....

"We are certainly not here to buy anything, Cynthia (whose looks and demeanour could well have impersonated an emaciated warthog) is going to do a course of ceramics at Farnham art college, so we've come to get some ideas, apparently you are quite well known ... however I did expect a little more salubrious establishment." Had I given up my afternoon for this.

He continued ... "Do you ever manage to sell any of this stuff?" Time to go to peasant mode. In my best Camborne brogue indeed unheard of for me I had not yet spoken. "Well Sur, we don't ave to"."What, why on earth not"."We be on work rehabilitation from the prison, up Exeter, great it be, no wardens an we can do as we like, nice pub down the road and the owner a bit simple like, could stay here for ever". "Good God, what the devil is this world coming to, disgusting. I shall get my land agent to file a complaint when I return to the estate, Cynthia we are leaving". "But Daddy I haven't had a proper look around" she simpers. "This is no place for you young lady, not to mix with these common people."

They leave ... I rapidly close and lock the door behind them. Thank you for coming, I obsequiously utter. Alas the heavens open, a heavy rainstorm erupts, he hammers on the door to be let back in, reiterating no taxi for half an hour ... Oh dear I didn't hear him ... Oh well what comes round goes round

As a member of the Devon and Cornwall police authority the week before I had been briefed on reintroducing past offenders back into the workforce. Never at the time thinking to use the experience to fully understand the problems facing the scheme first hand.

Hallucinations, 1998

Granite Seabirds, 1987

Rasta Man

Scillonian Naivety

AS MANY OF YOU will know, I have a passion for placing Bourdeaux pottery stickers in extremely random places. Sistine Chapel in Rome, Buckingham Palace in London and indeed several other notable places, always taking care to donate to charity so that usually no offence can be taken. It's quite fun to embarrass my children, and fun indeed to get messages from friends and customers who have spotted them in the strangest of places.

A few years ago I had an acquaintance who was a friend of the Governor General of a small Caribbean protectorate, while he was visiting with the governor he thought it would be fun, and in the spirit of the pottery to place a large John Bourdeaux pottery sticker on the Governor's Rolls Royce and drive to my son's place of work on the Island, and to watch his reaction. Unfortunately Ben was off Island so they decided to have a walk around the Marina where he worked. In passing they visited a small pottery workshop and had a fairly animated conversation about Island politics with the Caribbean owner called "tea pot" or so he told them. Also explaining in detail his Rastafarian roots and various other beliefs in certain herbal remedies he recommended, which were of no interest at all to them, and indeed maybe however well intended, by offering my friend some "good weed" could put him in some jeopardy.

However time to go, the Rolls with driver turned up, really impressing "tea pot" who, spotting the pottery sticker, immediately took a renewed interest in looking for a new member of staff who was an experienced potter. My friend extricating himself by passing on Ben's cell phone number.

Having had an email relating the story I determined to pay the studio a visit, with a view to offering my services for a couple of months, thus enabling us to spend some more Caribbean time with our younger son, we loved his lifestyle and his really great and welcoming friends, including a fantastic Scillonian family who have now returned to our own Islands.

Meanwhile "teapot" had been pestering Ben, as he also had a much coveted sticker on his car. We paid a visit to "tea pot's" studio to find that he actually couldn't make pots, but was proficient at glazing and firing, so we entered into a negotiation, he would provide accommodation for us both, and pay me on a peace work basis of five dollars a pot ... heavens above, I could make a fortune as being a production thrower, I can produce a pot in approximately two minutes.

I proudly showed off my skills, making a good pot for him in a very quick time ... His demeanour soon altered, withdrawing his original offer to one dollar a pot, and free herbal remedies ... no way ... However he now showed us the accommodation ... a shed with a sand floor, no windows and a latrine uncovered in the far corner.

"Really sorry,' I said, 'perhaps not" ... whatever other incentives he might offer.

Karma

Latin Coursework

HAVING SUFFERED A PUBLIC school education from the age of eight, it didn't take me long to work out that I wasn't destined for an Academic Career. One early school end of term report kindly suggesting that I should face up to my problems and difficulties and overcome them, rather than bypass them. Avoiding various academic problems such as maths and Latin coursework, had become the norm, indeed my sixpence a week collection was well spent, by a very clever move in paying one of the more academic and forward people to do my homework. This enterprising young person being extremely bright and slightly avaricious, gladly accepted the challenge, subject to the payment.

Obviously he was destined for a dynamic and successful career. On June 18 this year 2018 I was happily working in my studio, enjoying the company of the many friends and customers who frequent it, indeed they have supported the studio over the last 40 years, their encouragement and support has helped the studio gain an international reputation, with works being sold all over the world, indeed several hundred thousand works of art have now been sold and exported to places as far away as Antarctica.

Today an elderly gentleman tall and autocratic entered the studio, basically to ask the way to the local communal gardens, his pleasant shrew like wife dutifully following ten paces behind. Taking in my somewhat dowdy and impoverished appearance, (that is covered in clay and paint as most working artists are) he expletes surely you are not the Bourdeaux that went to prep school with me?

If you had worked harder and spent less time playing chess (I had played for the Cornwall senior team from the age of eleven) you could have now been retired as I am and be carrying one of these, (brandishing a black Amex card).

His pleasant wife looked embarrassed and indeed several of my regulars looked bewildered, particularly having read my last book (Tales of a travelling Potter, now on its fourth reprint) Kindly, the wife decided to help the struggling potter with a small purchase of three pounds ninety nine pence. The Amex was passed over and placed in the clay ridden card machine, no no need for a pin number, he paid ostentatiously with his new Apple watch. Oh to have such wealth.

Alas the card was declined much to the extreme enjoyment of all the audience. I then promptly cut the card in half with my clay ridden scissors, and threw it with a very apologetic glance in his direction into the waste paper bin, with all the other ceramic detritus. Total apoplexy ... A very very embarrassed and angry gentleman, albeit all this embarrassment for the princely sum of £3.99, the cost of a small ceramic shrew.

Smiling with a show of great sympathy for this financially embarrassed fellow, I offered to help him with his hotel bill as he only had the one card, he could pay me when he returned to Surrey by credit transfer. Thoroughly chastened he left the studio, I called to the pleasant wife handing her a black Amex card in perfect condition ... by sleight of hand I had switched cards and cut up one of my old cards that I used for smoothing clay.

It was in 1957 that I had last met this gentleman, I felt I still owed him a little, as indeed somehow I passed my common entrance to Public School. With his coursework help.

Lancashire Hotpot?

Different Commissions

SEVERAL YEARS AGO I had a contract to make urns, for a small funeral director in Torquay. These were always made with great humility and a respect for the final recipient.

When the contract ceased I had several surplus to requirements. Not wanting to capitalise on this, I discarded all pots onto a shard pile, however unbeknown to me a member of our extended family acquired one of these without permission, indeed the one chosen had been used and returned as the incumbent had spilled slightly, due to a faulty lid.

Approximately six months later we were invited to dinner with these extended relations, I seemed to lose my appetite when the Lancashire hotpot was served in the funeral urn.

I was for once speechless.

Several times over the past few years I have repeated the story albeit with several embellishments and indeed this has led to several interesting and different commissions. Indeed I have been privileged to make with humour and love several delightful pieces to store various individual's ashes. I should add that all recipients I knew well, and indeed I think they would've been delighted with the memorials, which have included a monkey a crocodile and a large tawny owl.

Last year a dear friend passed away, she was always full of fun with a passion for swimming, Scilly and seals. The family had come to Scilly to scatter her ashes, a fairly sad occasion for us all. I was asked tentatively if I could find a happy solution as a memory of our dear friend. So with love and humour as always we used some of the ashes mixed with my clay to make a set of seals for all the family to remember their loved one for years to come, all this occurred because of a well cooked Lancashire hotpot. What next I wonder? Grandad in a teapot?

Self Portrait

Angels and MJ6

The Potter and the Bomb Squad

IN 1974 WHEN THE Prime Minister of the day was clinging to power in the liberal labour pact I was nearly in great trouble with M16 and the bomb squad.

Lady Wilson, a regular visitor and customer had spied a nativity set I was making for the 1984 Christmas season, Lady Mary as always thinking outside the box, that is not purchasing the whole set but commissioning twelve porcelain angels at the great expense of 20p each. Delighted to receive this prestigious order I duly completed it, individually gift wrapped and sent to the Wilson's private address in Ashley Gardens in London.

A few days later at eight am, there was a loud knocking on the studio door, who on earth could that be at this time in the morning. To my amazement two fairly sombre policemen stood there, they themselves not too happy at the early hour ... however important the business. And a separate call from no 10 had put them on their metal. "What have you sent to 16 Ashley Gardens... ?"

I replied in all naivety and innocence "Angels". "Don't be bloody stupid ... what have you sent", the Irascible Sergeant demands. I explained that I actually had sent twelve tinfoil gift wrapped angels to Lady Mary.

Apparently MI6 had intercepted the parcel, the tinfoil setting off the security systems and the bomb squad had been summoned, as at that time the Irish Republican Army were in full flow, in a letter bombing campaign.

My angels survived and indeed only a few years ago Lady Mary laughingly recalled the incident, when choosing a present for Sarah Brown having been invited to Chequers for the weekend … "No tinfoil in the packing this time please" she chuckled.

Classic Jugs, 2018

Coffee Time

28th June 1980

WELL ANOTHER LOVELY DAY here on St Mary's, the pottery is beginning to pay its way. Work at six thirty each day helps to have plenty of time to stop and have enlivening conversations with all my fantastic customers and friends.

This morning a continental family of four entered my unique establishment. The male of the species introduced himself as Heinrich with his wife Geisla repeating most of his words, very proud of their language skills and certainly not reticence in asking questions, indeed I could well be being interrogated by Herr Flick. "Ow moche is de mug of coffee".

I am very proud of my new range of granite ware, so with absolute confidence I reply with a price of five pounds and would happily accept a little less for a purchase of two or more. What I can only describe as an outburst, Heinrich in faltering English exclaims. "U are de rogue in Penzance dey is only seventy five pence". Sorry I surprisingly exclaim, it's a very complex process taking many hours and are totally unique to this pottery.

Somewhat pacified, "ver do ve sit", well, wherever you like sadly we have no chairs but you are welcome to sit on the step, albeit having a covering of dusty clay. "Bring us de menu then". This is really getting out of hand, as although normally of a passive nature his demands seemed unbelievable.

I followed however with an up-to-date price list of all my ceramic wares. He remonstrated that I did not deserve his custom, my coffee was extortionate and indeed who would eat puffins, shags and wrens. Still bewildered I was summoned to my new advertising board on the main thorofare. Alas I at last understood his anger and confusion.

Open 10-12 noon. Lunch 12 - 1pm. Afternoon opening 1 - 4pm.

What's in a notice ... ?

In my country he tells me without any humour, when you advertise de lunch it means you serve food for us people to eat. Sadly a confused continental left the studio without buying the extortionate mug of de coffee. I immediately altered the sign, hopefully no more misunderstandings.

Osprey in granite glaze, 1983

Robertus Hayesus

A Challenge Not to Disappoint

A DYNAMIC YOUNG NORTHERNER who arrived on the Islands several years ago, caused me great embarrassment on one memorable day in June 2018.

Robertus has been a great asset to the Islands, successfully stewarding the local golf course, running a fantastic guest house and being an outstanding artist in his own right, although to be fair one could call his masterpieces somewhat "wooden"! As a man of leisure he has spent the last two seasons helping in a prestigious art gallery centrally situated in Hugh Town, St Marys.

To avoid the boredom on quiet days, together with some of his patrons, he decided to enliven my days by offering various incentives to visit my establishment. Some patrons totally unaware of the prank ... others all too aware ... One free cream tea and two hour talk on the intricacy of ceramic modelling read one, whilst another offered a two hour talk on Rhinos (one of my latest sculptures). These beautifully written offers arriving fairly frequently, leaving me to work out how to deal with the diverse recipients. Indeed a challenge to not disappoint, while actually not providing any of the fictitious offers. I in turn, reciprocated by parcelling up various items of ceramic and other detritus to be returned to Robertus.

He only once had to remonstrate with me, as by mistake a delightful lady struggled to carry an iron bar to him, that I had gilded and described as treasure from the wreck of The Association in 1707. "The poor woman was so excited to perform this task, that I feared for her health" commented Robertus. However all went well with this light hearted banter ... until ... June 16th 2018. A date I shall never forget ... The studio was full of customers, most of whom I knew well. When a very tall, extremely thin lady arrived, she was the picture of an upper class Roedean girl, probably sixty years old, with a great resemblance to an elongated turkey, indeed with a voice to match.

"Are you the potter chap" she bellows. Covered in clay from head to foot really didn't need an answer, however in true servility and civility I affirmed that I indeed was the "potter chap"."Well I'm a ceramicist from Winchester, and I would like a tour of this pottery." Taking out a notebook and pen she proceeded to ask me the minerals and techniques involved in my lustreware (which I had been developing over the past twenty years, indeed a closely guarded secret) How did I give a polite refusal without giving offence?

Suddenly realising Robertus had once again broken through my urbane defences, I decided in this instance attack was the best form of defence, indeed I was going to miss a sale today with this latest intrusion. Robertus must have used all his charm to get this upper class if not titled lady to take part. As I had a good audience I decided to turn the tables immediately on Robertus so that his windup would backfire.

With a defined wink at the ten or so customers gathered, I bade Lady Sybil (she had just informed us of her pedigree, confirming my earlier assumptions) that if she could pop out into the drying shed, (adjacent to the studio) take off all her clothes and I would be with her forthwith.

Alas not the response I and my customers expected ... Robertus had not sent her, she was genuine!!! I shall never forget the look of horror and shock on her face ... I tried to explain ... showing her the reward cards that are usually proffered with these requests, but in my embarrassment my hands started shaking uncontrollably. Desperately trying to stabilise the misunderstanding I proffered an inscribed pen of the pottery ... with logo. Blankly refusing this prestigious gift, she left the studio, never to return ... At least, hopefully not.

Fishwife, 2012

Misdirection?

A Thursday in July

TODAY IS A THURSDAY in July, a lovely sunny day, I've had a great morning, really lovely people, lots of conversation and reminiscences, in fact all is good, if the world ended tomorrow I wouldn't unduly complain. Too good to last?

I am quietly having my lunch 1pm - 2pm, The studio doorbell is ringing incessantly, someone must be in trouble, I rush to help. I am accosted by a fiftyish, Amazonian woman who informs me in no uncertain terms that "you locals, don't deserve to earn a living". She certainly had no time to wait while I had a lunch break.

Not defending myself I abjectly apologised and opened up the studio for her, especially so as she had come from a cruise ship docked in the St Mary's roads off Tresco, and indeed she informed me she had a premier suite and had dined with the charming Lithuanian Captain the night before.

However a purchase was far from her autocratic mind, she was desperate to find the large pottery that she visited on the last cruise, I apologetically explained that indeed I was the only pottery still on the Island. "Don't try and fool me" she exclaimed. "I came here to your Island and purchased a beautiful pot" She showed me the catalogue of the very nice pot that she had purchased last year, and indeed showed me in no uncertain terms at my attempt to bamboozle her, and to try and sell her one of mine.

No point in continuing this pointless conversation, indeed she did have the catalogue. I reluctantly gave her the directions to the pottery she had sought. "Go to the top of the road and turn right, and then keep walking" She stormed off with a very self satisfied look on her face, no acknowledgement or thank you.

I'm not sure how long she walked, as indeed the pottery she sought, was in Guernsey in the Channel Islands ... several hundred miles away. I indeed felt assured that at least technically I had given her the answer she wanted. I then returned to finish my lunch and decided to break my 'no drinking' rule at lunchtimes and to have a nice glass of wine.

Totem, 2017

August

If the Cap Fits

HAVING JUST PASSED THROUGH several months where the majority of our customers are retired, or in their sixties, seventies and eighties, it comes as quite a dramatic shock to meet the changing clientele that August brings. Delightful young families, many of whom the parents themselves have come as children and are enjoying the nostalgia of their own childhood.

These are the norm, however they are interspersed with slightly fraught grandparents, who apart from baby sitting duties, and paying for the holiday, find life slightly stressful having to share with a son in law or daughter in law, who have totally differing ideas of what family life should involve ... whilst the youngsters themselves, despite the grandparents' help question the fact as to why us upwardly mobile young people have to put up with these politically incorrect Neanderthals.

Not really a holiday made in heaven ... however when they finally depart to the happy hunting grounds, hopefully the sale of their four bed semi, will pay off our own mortgage, and give us a better way of life.

This puts great stress on the aforesaid partner, who actually loves these old people, and urges them to enjoy life, and spend their inheritance, but for Gods' sake don't go into a residential home, as that would be disastrous for their own monetary future.

Then we have the rapid breeders, quite often with three to four precocious children, all being privately educated, Daddy working all hours in the city, leaving home at six am and returning late at night. Probably having an intense affair with one of his adoring secretaries, due to the lack of attention from the male or indeed female breadwinner, who is probably horizontally jogging with the personal trainer. The point of this story is that on holiday, not being used to the confines of a close family unit, they continually bicker and complain about most things they encounter. Perhaps a branch of Relate could be opened for the month of August?

Just while writing this, a very precocious twelve year old has entered the studio with his adoring mother, they continue a conversation in very loud voices about the family in the next time share, apparently extremely well off, but unlike Daddy and I they don't have a property in Rock, (the Cornish resort for the rich and famous) explains the overbearing mother.

Slightly distracted by me the peasant potter who has just had the audacity to interrupt their conversation, to say a happy good morning. The objectionable twelve year old looks at me with a mixture of superiority and disdain ... "How much do you think this bloke earns in a day". "Well ask him" said Lucrezia Borgia. Unprompted ... I interject ... "Probably about ten years for manslaughter" I mutter ... alas they left the studio, never I hope to return.

However ninety nine per cent of August visitors are fantastic happy people, we just hope they keep coming to our beautiful islands, and don't get put off by the very small minority that don't really fit into our classless and simple way of life.

Wait a minute ... a very dominant lady has just entered the studio, she really does typify a certain breed of the minority that frequent our paradise Islands ... she knows everyone ...

misinterprets the local gossip ... idolises all the local boatmen, referring to them by their Christian names whenever possible ... indeed the font of all Scillonian knowledge.

Today she has decided to show all the local galleries to her friend who is visiting the Islands for the first time. I suppose you could sum up the encounter as patronisingly critical ... she spies a rather splendid Rhinoceros that I have just proudly finished after several months work ... alas not to her liking ... "What a ridiculous thing to make, nothing to do with the islands".

"Surely" I interrupt "Have you not heard of the proposed Rhino sanctuary that is hopefully being set up with the aid of European grant money on one of the off islands?" Not wishing to show her lack of local knowledge, she replies, "Of course I have". "Well perhaps you might like to pop into the relevant office in the town hall and make a donation". With that several customers entered the studio, and she, left as always avoiding any possible chance of buying even the smallest of items to support the studio. Sadly leaving before I could enlighten her of the hoax ...

Apparently she spent the next week, complaining to all she met about her absolute disgust at the waste of European grant on such an animal ... even to the extent of contacting the local councillor, who rang me with great amusement, enclosing a non-committal letter to the complainant, saying that if such an event ever occurred he would take her views into account. Who knows? Maybe next year a casino on Samson, or an open prison on St Helens?

Coffee Pot, 1990

Teapot, Abstracted, 2010

Mistaken Identity

The Colonel's Wife

MANY YEARS AGO BEFORE holiday homes became prevalent it was a fairly rare experience to welcome new permanent residents. In those days we knew everyone, so that any new member of the community was welcomed with a slight amount of caution and in turn the new residents kept a fairly low profile and slowly integrated into our fairly insular but welcoming community.

In those days both churches on the island were thriving, sadly unlike today, so the new residents chose their places of worship making their mark with their new friends.

I myself, although an Anglican, was privileged to play in the chapel band. A brass band encompassing young and old. A wonderful bond of friendship encompassed us all.

One particular Sunday the minister Bob Dunstan called me aside to introduce two new members of the congregation – a Colonel Reid and his diminutive wife. They had started to settle in really well without ruffling many feathers, quite a feat in those xenophobic days, real pillars of the community in the making. Chapel choir, theatre club and hints of wanting to join the bench as a magistrate.

I promised to do my best and suggested they pop into the studio and we could have a good chat and get better acquainted.

A few weeks later I had a call from the local police sergeant warning me of a serious outbreak of shoplifting on the Islands.

Mainly perpetrated by some youths camping at Pelistry, a rare occurrence as usually these groups of people were well disciplined and a model of well behaved young people. A couple of hours later I was invaded by approximately twenty young campers, all acting suspiciously, and probably about to do some serious shoplifting.

I decided to act immediately and stop these giggling youngsters before they could act. One long-haired individual caught my attention, handling all the pots and then discarding them.

I walked quickly through the throng deciding to make an example of this individual, promptly lifting him up by the scruff of his anorak and bodily taking him to the door, in a loud voice saying, 'out ... and, please don't come back ...' it worked and the rest of the customers went into a stunned silence ... with the exception of one adolescent who had the nerve to laugh.

I was just about to remonstrate with him, when he pointed delightedly to the door ... and there stood the diminutive and astonished Mrs Reid!

Oh dear, a clear case of mistaken identity!

I had expelled her with some force out of the studio. After grovelling apologies she left ... returning with her husband the next day ... laughingly asking if it was okay for her to come in for a look around.

A lovely lady, luckily with a great sense of humour.

The Power Cut

And Bits & Bobs

HERE WE ARE IN the middle of August and the local power company has had to replace some power cables. This is fairly disastrous for our small business. However trying to make the most of a bad job, we installed numerous candles, a manual credit card machine, and set out to try and get a few sales. The studio looked fairly romantic, but alas very difficult to see the paintings and pottery. Several people briefly looked in the door but soon rapidly left.

However there was to be some light in our darkness ... a very attractive nubile young lady called 'Alison' entered the studio ... I had met her several times over the past few years, with her quiet and self-effacing friend. An extremely pleasant young man, who was obviously captivated by this human dynamo of womanhood. We were having a serious discussion on the aerodynamics of a concord sculpture that I had recently finished, when I noticed our young lady filling her rucksack with several vases and a small puffin ... with that they shook hands and left ... what was I to do?

Perhaps I should send the bill to the power company ... Ring the Police? No, just put it down to another experience in life ... She certainly shouldn't go to court for such a small offence. Indeed I am truly flattered that she found my humble wares good enough to purloin. Happy travels Alison ... you are always welcome at the studio.

Totem, 2005

Ceramic Imprints

August 21st, 2017

ONE OF THE GREAT advantages of being an ageing potter in the Isles of Scilly, is that due to your way of life etc, you cannot be classified in any of the obvious ways to discern your status in this sad materialistic world.

Hence you are usually no threat to anyone, and accordingly people lose some of their inhibitions while frequenting the studio. This is wonderful for the craftsman, so he builds really strong bonds with his customers who become good friends.

Today however all did not go exactly as planned ... a very attractive young lady whom I have known for many years came into the studio to say hello ... she wanted to introduce her new partner, inconsequentially ... about twenty years her senior. However he was reticent to come in and be introduced. Indeed he asked her to be as quick as possible so that he could ravage a pint at the local hostelry.

Slightly embarrassed by his behaviour which I had obviously overheard, she came in full flow behind the counter to emphatically give me a more demonstrative hug than normal. Probably over-emphasised due to the circumstances ... who was I, an ageing scruffy potter, to complain?

However ... I had spent the morning making about fifty large pots on the wheel and consequently was covered in wet clay all over the front of my apron.

During the embrace the fine earthen ware porcelain mix had transferred to the ample accoutrements of the young lady ... with clay hand prints on her back ... a true Faulty Towers moment ... not comprehending her situation she said goodbye blew a kiss and left the studio.

The ensuing conversation with her new sugar daddy is not suitable for this fine publication.

From my point of view ... innocence is Bliss!!!

A work in progress ... Feb. 1978

Also Available

TALES *of a*
TRAVELLING POTTER

John Bourdeaux

from
John Bourdeaux,
The Pottery, Old Town,
St Mary's, Isles of Scilly.
bourdeauxpottery@gmail.com.
01720422025
www.johnbourdeauxpottery.co.uk